Contents

Introduction

This beverage, originating in Asia, has been consumed for centuries, and thanks to careful plant breeding, the development of scores of harvesting and processing techniques, and regional differences in climate and environment, there are hundreds of varieties of tea available on the market today. And that's just real tea that made with the leaves of Camellia sinensis if you add in tisanes, made from herbs, the possibilities are virtually endless.

Lots of tea lovers keep a large supply of tea varietals at home, some of which may include rare or hard to find specialties like pu-erh from China. But did you know that you can actually grow and process your own tea, and maintain a tea and tisane garden for making custom blends of teas that tickle your fancy? Not only will a tea garden save you a ton of money on tea, it can also look gorgeous, and it might be a striking conversation piece especially if you situate a lovely tiled patio in the middle of it so you can enjoy tea and snacks on warm days.

While there are lots of ways to lay out a tea garden, one option is to choose a classic quartered theme like that seen in many English gardens. This style, with a central area and four pathways bordering four beds, has a nice formal look to it, but it also provides easy access to all the beds. You could also consider a spiral, which would allow you to walk along one arm of the spiral to harvest and work on plants located on the other arm.

What is a Tea Garden?

A tea garden is a place to grow your favourite herbs for tea, and much more. Tea herbs are visually a

Appealing and delightfully fragrant.

What to plant?

Well, if you want to be classic, you'll need some tea plants. These shrubs grow outdoors in zones seven through nine, reaching a height of around four feet. They like full sun, lots of nutrients, and well-drained but moist soil, so plan around this when determining where to plant them. The University of Hawaii has an excellent guide for picking and processing basic black and green teas which can be used as a starting point for developing your own custom varietals.

That's just the beginning, though. Some common ingredients in flavored teas or tisanes without any tea in them include:

lemon, orange, lemon verbena, oregano, chamomile, mint, dandelions, blackberries, hibiscus, ginger, rosemary, fenugreek, echinacea, anise, raspberry leaves, licorice, jasmine, lavender, clover, violet, chrysanthemum, yerba buena, spearmint, coriander, beebalm, rose hips, dock leaves, ginseng, chicory, pine needles, yarrow, willow bark or twigs, sarsaparilla, sassafras, and many more. Check out your own pantry and the herbal teas shelf at the local market for inspiration.

You may note that many of these plants are attractive flowering plants, trees, and shrubs. Some, like blackberries and raspberries, produce fruit in addition to useful leaves. You can use all of this to your advantage as you weave together a garden plan that will include a variety of delicious ingredients you can use to make your own teas and tisanes.

Develop a list of things you'd like to grow and research them in resources to determine whether they will grow where you live and what kinds of conditions they like. Take special note of things that require a lot of space or special growing conditions; for example, if you want to grow willows, they like a lot of water. You might be able to accommodate them with a pond in your tea garden that would create a nice sitting area to relax, drink tea, and enjoy the environment...but if you live in a hot, dry climate, you might want to skip the willow.

 Map out your tea garden precisely with everything you want to grow, and start establishing seedlings or planting seeds after the last chance of frost to give your plants a chance to get started. You'll need to water and fertilize regularly in the first two years to allow the garden to get established (and some tea ingredients are annuals, so they'll need to be replaced after producing flowers, leaves, and roots). Nervous about this phase? Talk to an Atlanta landscaping company about planning out a garden and helping you with maintenance as you get starts.

 As plants mature, take advantage of the opportunity to dry ingredients so you'll have access to them all year. Drying racks are simple and easy to set up (unused window screens can work in a pinch), and you can store your ingredients in bags, tins, or jars in a cool, dry, dark place so they'll maintain freshness over the cold winter months when you want a breath of fresh air and a reminder of your spring and summer garden.

Climate and soil

Tea is exacting in its climatic requirements. The temperature may vary from 16 to 320C and annual rainfall should be 125 to 150 cm, which is well distributed over 8-9 months in a year. The atmospheric humidity should be always around 80% during most of the time. Very dry atmosphere is not congenial for tea. It is grown in plains in North Eastern States but in South India, it is grown in hill ranges from 600 to 2200 m above M.S.L.

Tea is a calcifuge crop requiring comparatively low amounts of calcium but high quantities of potassium and silicon. They can be grown in lateritic, alluvial and peaty soils. Optimum pH range is 4.5 to 5.0 and soil depth should be 1.0 to 1.5m.

Propagation

Tea can be propagated by seed and by cuttings. Seeds collected from the fruits of seed baries are soaked in water and only heavy seeds, which sink, are alone used for sowing in beds. Germination occurs in 20 to 30 days. At that stage they are carefully lifted and transplanted in polythene sleeves. They will be ready for planting in 9 months.

Vegetative propagation

The site for the nursery can be selected in a flat land or gentle slope, near to a perennial water source and easily accessible by road. It should have a good drainage and should be protected from wind, frost and wild animals etc. approximately, 0.15 ha nursery area is required to produce 1.25 lakhs cuttings. Nursery area is to be provided with overhead shade by erecting concrete or stone pillars at a spacing of 3x3m and spread with 6mm2 mesh double strand coirmat which provides about 67% shade.

The cuttings for rooting are collected from mother bushes, which are well maintained near the nursery area. Such mother bushes are pruned well in advance to induce juvenile shoots. These juvenile shoots are collected in the morning hours and 3cm long cutting each with a healthy mother leaf and an active axillary bud is prepared.

Cuttings from top tender and bottom brown wood should be avoided. These cuttings are planted in polythene bags (30cmx10cmx150 gauge), filled with growing medium (Jungle soil: river sand 3:1) in the bottom and rooting medium (Red/subsoil:sand 1:1) in the top 8-10cm. The soil used for rooting media should have an optimum pH range of 4.8 to 5.0, if high, i.e., 5.1 to 5.5, or 5.6 to 6.0, it must be drenched with

1 or 2% aluminum sulphate solution respectively at 1 litre per cubic foot of soil. This treatment should follow with drenching of twice the volume of plain water to wash excess aluminum sulphate.

The cuttings are carefully planted at the centre of the bags in such a way that the petiole should not touch the soil and then they are watered. These bags are then covered with polythene sheets over the G.I. wire arhes and the sides are tugged well to preserve moisture content. Callusing starts in 4-6 weeks and rooting occurs in 10 to 12 weeks. When 80% of the cuttings have rooted, the tents are opened in stages and the overhead shade is gradually reduced to harden the plants.

Planting

The land is cleared of the roots of the fallen trees and drains are taken at suitable intervals depending upon the slope to conserve the soil. In the olden days, up and down system of planting at 1.2x1.2m are followed. Presently, contour planting either in a single hedge or double hedge system is followed. Sr. No. Type Spacing Population/ha.

- Up and down 1.2 x 1.2m 6,800
- Contour planting single hedge. 1.2 x 0.75m 10,800

- Contour planting double hedge. 1.35 x 0.75 x 0.75m 13,200

The last method has many advantages over the first two viz., early and high yield, better soil conservation, less weed growth in the hedge and efficient cultural practices. Planting season normally coincides with June/July and September/October for SouthWest monsoon and North East monsoon areas. Pits of 30x30x45cm size are dug and plants of 12-15 months old are planted by removing the polythene sleeves. Immediate after planting, plants are staked to prevent wind damage.

After care

Immediately after planting, the soil surface around the plants should be mulched, usually cutgrasses of gautemala are employed for this purpose. About 25 tonnes of grass is required to mulch one hectare. Care must be taken to keep the mulch materials away from the collar region last they may cause collar diseases. If there is a dry weather, mud tubes or etah tubes may be buried 15cm deep near the plant in a slanting position and one litre of water per plant may be poured or injected at weekly intervals. This subsoil irrigation helps to minimise the causality besides encourages developing deeper roots.

Shade management

Tea requires filtered shade and if it is exposed to direct sun, its growth is affected. Shade is hence essential and beneficial to tea as:

- It regulates the temperature.
- It minimises the effects of drought and radiation injury.
- It increases the soil fertility
- It helps in recycling of nutrients.
- It helps in getting even distribution of crop.
- It serves as windbreak.
- It reduces the incidences of pests.
- It generates additional income by way of timber and fuel.
- The desirable characters of a good shade tree like
- It must be an evergreen tree, easy to propagate having quick growing and deep rooted characters.
- It provides filtered shade and withstands frequent lopping.

- It tolerates wind and frost.
- It does not have allopathic effect.
- It has commercial timber value also.

Weed control

Weeds will be a problem in young and pruned fields. Manual weeding is never recommended in tea lest more soil erosion and damage to surface roots and collar regions. Therefore, the following chemical weed control is alone recommended in tea.

Type of weeds Herbicides Dosage:

- Dicots Paraquat (gramoxone) 1.12 lit. /ha.
- Dicots Sodium salt of 2,4-D (Fernoxone) 1.4 kg. /ha.
- Grasses 2,2-Dichloro propionic acid (Dalapon) 5.6 kg. /ha.
- Glyphosate 2.3 lit. /ha.

Training and Pruning

In the young tea, when it has established well, centering i.e. removing the growing point leaving 8 to 10 mature leaves from the bottom, is done to induce secondaries. When the secondaries reach more than 60 cm, they are tipped at 50-55 cm height by removing 3 to 4 leaves and bud to induce tertiaries. Therefore, plucking at mother leaf stage is continued for better frame development. It takes nearly 18 to 20 months from planting to reach regular plucking field stage.

 Pruning is done in tea:

- to maintain to convenient height for plucking
- to induce more vegetative growth
- to remove dead and de funct wood and
- to remove the knots and interlaced branches.

Pruning is normally done 4 to 6 years interval depending upon the altitude of the garden, nature of the materials etc. the bushes marked for pruning should have adequate starch reserves in roots otherwise the sprouting following pruning should have adequate starch reserves in roots otherwise the sprouting following pruning will be less. This can be normally tested by the common Iodine test and if the starch reserve is less, bushes are allowed to rest for 2 to 3 months. The different types of pruning are as follows: -

- Sr. N. Type of pruning Pruning height (cm) Season Remarks
- Rejuvenation pruning 20 – China Jat,

- Assam Jat April - May Done is old bushes affected with cankar and wood rot to invigorate the new healthy branches. Not done regularly.
- Hard pruning 30 – 45 Apr. – May First formative pruning done to a young tea.
- Medium pruning 45 – 60 Aug. – Sept. Normal pruning whereever frames are healthy.
- Light pruning 60 – 65 Aug. – Sept. Normal pruning whereever frames are healthy.
- Skiffing 65 Aug. – Sept. Mainly to postpone pruning and to encourage better frame development.

Immediately after the rejuvenation or hard pruning, the cut ends are smeared with a paste made of copper oxychloride and linseed oil (1:1). The prunings, consisting of only small twings and leaves are buried in trenches of 30cm width and 45cm depth taken across the slope in alternate rows. The pruned bushes are given washing with 10% lime solution using No. IV nozzle of power sprayers in order to kill the epiphytic growth of moss and lichen so as to induce early and even bud break. Lime washing also minimises sunscorch to the bush frame.

The buds from the pruned shoots grow in a steady succession without any cessation of growth. These are known as a periodic shoots or primary shoots. These primary shoots should be induced to produce flush shoots, otherwise known as periodic shoots by regular tipping operation. Tipping is the removal of terminal portion of the shoot and it varies with jats and pruning height as given below. Tipping height refers to the number of leaves that must be left above the pruned cut while tipping in material refers to that portion of the terminal shoot, which must be tipped off.

Manures And Fertilisers

Tea responds to manuring and it has been estimated that to produce 100kg of made tea, tea plant utilises on an average 10.2, 3.2 and 5.4kg of Nitrogen, Phosphorus and Potash per ha. Manuring in tea starts from nursery stage itself. Once they strike roots (after 4 months) 30g of soluble mixtures (Ammonium phosphate (20:20) 35 parts, potassium sulphate and Magnesium sulphate each 15 parts and zinc sulphate and Magnesium sulphate each 15 parts and zinc sulphate – 3 parts) is dissolved in 10 litres of water and is applied with rosecan for about 900 plants. This must be repeated at 15 days intervals.

- Nitrogen

The recommendation for mature tea is based mostly on soil organic matter status and anticipated yield. For a field with medium organic matter status the following rates of application is suggested for every 100kg of made tea anticipated:

Yield level (kg/ha) Rate of Nitrogen (for 100 kg. of made tea) No. of split applications

- <3000 10 kg 4
- 3000 8 kg 5
- 3000 and above 9 kg 6

Twenty per cent of the total nitrogen is given in the form of Ammonium sulphate during March/April. Urea is recommended in May/June and receding monsoon months avoiding very wet and very dry periods and it will come to 65% of total nitrogen. Fifteen percent of the total nitrogen is applied in the form of Calcium Ammonium Nitrate during pre-winter (November-December).

- Potassium

Nitrogen and potassium are always applied together. NK ratio of 1:1 is used for plucking fields while for a pruned field 2:3

NK ratio is recommended. For rejuvenation pruned field 1:2 NK ratio is suggested. The enhanced rates of potassium application in the pruned year is to encourage formation of healthy farmers. Muriate of potash is the sources of potassium used in tea fields. The NK fertilizers are applied by broadcast for mature tea and is broadcast and dibbled in along the drip circle for young tea. The interval between two successive applications should be atleast 3-4 weeks.

- Phosphorus

Phosphorus is applied once in alternate years , 90kg P2O5/ha for fields yielding less than 3000kg/ha for fields yielding between 3000 and 4500kg/ha, 60 to 80kg P2O5/ha is suggested every year. The soils being acidic, rock phosphate could be advantageously used. The fertilizer should be placed at 15-22cm depth.

- Micronutrients

Among the micronutrients, zinc deficiency is often manifested in young shoots characterised by reduced leaf size, rosetting, chlorosis and formation of more banji shoots. Application of zinc sulphate, 6 to 8kg/ha for high yielding fields every year is the general recommendation. The above quantity can be given in 4 to 5 split applications during has been found beneficial to combine other micronutirents viz., Manganese sulphate, 15.5g/10 litres and boric acid, 5.5g/10 litres of spray volume along with zinc sulphate spray.

- Liming

In the hill soils, due to the leaching of bases by rain and also due to the incessant application of acid forming fertilizers, the soil pH is often reduced which affects the physical and chemical properties of soil. Therefore, periodical application of lime is essential properties of soil. Therefore, periodical application of lime is essential to amend the soil and maintain optimum pH. Agricultural lime (Calcium carbonate) and dolomitic lime (Calcium Magnesium carbonate) are generally recommended for tea soils. The rate of application is based on soil pH, rainfall, fertilizer usage and length of the pruning cycle. Roughly lime, 1.5mt/ha for a pH between 4.5 to 4.9, 3.0mt/ha for a pH between 4.0 to 4.4 and 4.0mt/ha for a pH of less than 4.0 is suggested.

The lime is applied by evenly broadcasting prior to pruning once in a pruning cycle. First manuring following liming can be had after 6 weeks and a minimum of 15cm rainfall should have been received during this period.

Harvesting or Plucking

Plucking consists of harvesting 2 to 3 leaves and a bud. It is the most labour intensive operation in a tea industry and also decides the yield and quality of made tea. Normally, a pluckable shoot takes 60 to 90 days for harvesting since its sprouting from the axillary buds. When the shoot is plucked upto mother leaf, it is known as light plucking and if it is plucked below mother leaf, it is called hard plucking. The plucking interval and plucking standard in relation to cropping is given below:

Cropping pattern Months Plucking interval

High cropping or Rush cropping (60% of total crop) April – June and October – December 7 – 10 days

Low cropping or lean cropping (40% of total crop) July – September and

January – March 12 –15 days

It is essential to add one tier of active maintenance foliage to the bush every year. This is done by mother leaf plucking during January to March. During the rest of the period level plucking can be carried out.

Consequent to plucking, bush height increases every year in the order of 10cm over tipping height in the first year, 7.5cm, 7.5cm, 5cm and 5cm over the previous year height in the second, third, fourth and fifth year respectively.

Yield

Yield of made tea per hectare depends upon many factors such as elevation, clonal or seedling jats, management practices, severity of pruning, processing techniques etc., Generally, in tea industry, a field which yields upto 2000kg of made tea/ha is considered as low yielding and 2000 to 3000kg as medium yielding and anything above 3000kg as high yielding fields.

The Tea Plant, Camellia sinensis

Whilst there are many different types of tea available on the supermarket shelf, most originate from the 'Tea Plant', otherwise known as Camellia Sinensis variant Sinensis.

Camellia sinensis is a hardy evergreen plant boasting glossy green, pointed and fragrant leaves. The appearance of delicate white flowers in the autumn means that this shrub has more to offer than just a refreshing cuppa. If you can grow other varieties of Camellia in your garden chances are you'll be able to grow Camellia sinensis.

The tea plant, or Camellia sinensis, is the plant from which tea is made. Tea leaves contain caffeine, and the leaves can be processed in different ways to produce different kinds of teas. Any brewed tea including Camellia sinensis is a proper tea, while those without Camellia sinensis usually made from mixtures of herbs and flowers are tisanes.

This plant prefers hardiness zones seven through nine and rich, moist environments with a lot of rainfall. Gardens located in moderate zones will be able to grow tea plants outdoors, while those in colder environments might consider keeping their tea plants in greenhouses, or pots for easy movement to insulated spaces come winter.

Despite its variety, all tea comes from the same plant. Whether it's white, green, oolong, black, or something more intense, such as pu-erh tea, all of it is made of the leaves of the Camellia sinensis plant. Perhaps even more surprising is that variances in flavor are generally not attributed to the way the plant is raised, not to the part of the plant used in tea-making (almost all tea is made using the leaves), but in how the leaves are processed on their journey between stem and cup. A less common type of tea, twig tea, is made using the woody parts (think stems and branches) of the tea plant as opposed to the leaves.

While many people drink tea for its complex, intriguing bouquet of flavors or the antioxidants, others sip tea for its pick-me-up caffeine boost. If you're looking for some extra mental energy, then aim for darker teas. It is the processing that causes teas to oxidize and become caffeinated.

Here are some of the processes you'll need to know when harvesting from your tea plants.

- Collecting: Use gardening shears or sharp scissors to snip freshly grown leaves from the ends of your tea plant.

- Withering: This is the process of allowing the leaves to air-dry. Usually leaves are withered in a thin layer on a flat tray.

- Rolling: using your hand or a cloth, roll the leaves so they're wrinkled. Rolling cracks the cell walls of the leaves and allows the flavors and antioxidants to escape into your brew.

- Drying: While tea can be served after it has been rolled, it is often more economic to spend your time producing enough tea for several brews. To store your tea for later use, you'll want to dry it. You can dry your tea by spreading it out in a thin layer to air dry, then lay it out in the sun—or you can bake it under low heat until the moisture is gone from the leaves.

If you want to add some caffeinated kick to your brews, you'll need to use some Camellia sinensis in your recipe. When harvesting from your tea plant, fresh, tender leaves are best for brewing. Depending on how processed the leaves are, various types of tea can be brewed.

- White Tea

White tea has generally undergone minimal processing between harvest and consumption. To prepare white tea leaves, snip freshly grown leaves from the end of your tea plant's branches, then let them air out away from the sun for a couple of days. Be sure to allow plenty of space and not pile them up so the moisture can evaporate and not grow mold.

- Green Tea

When people think of hot tea, a freshly brewed cup of green tea often comes to mind. Green tea is very convenient because it can be consumed the same day it is harvested. To prepare green tea,snip fresh leaves from your tea plant and again let them air dry for a while—approximately seven hours. At this point, heat the leaves briefly in a frying pan, then roll the leaves. Your tea is now ready to steep and brew.

- Oolong Tea

For oolong tea, the leaves must first undergo wilting for a couple days. To allow for oxidation, the leaves must then be shaken several times in a span of about 30 minutes between each shaking. After this process, the leaves are ready to be rolled.

- Black Tea

Black tea requires trial and error. Depending on your tea plant and your environment, the leaves may need a longer or shorter wilting period after harvest. While rolling leaves for black tea, more pressure is necessary than for other types of tea. You will know your leaves have been sufficiently rolled when juice starts to come out of the leaves.

The last step before serving or storing is to allow the leaves to rest in a warm place until they change color to that rich, warm red-brown black tea leaves boast. Again, depending on your tea plant and the environment you're working in, the time it takes can vary drastically, sometimes as little as a few hours are necessary, and sometimes half a day. It will require trial and error and a watchful eye for you to learn what the exact process is to produce your best cup of tea.

Whichever type of tea or tisane you prefer, you're bound to find the process of growing and harvesting your own cup rewarding. Use this guide to help you in selecting the types best for your taste and your environment. Then relax with a cup of freshly prepared tea you can trace every step of the way from leaf to brew.

Varieties of Tea Plant

The natural habitat of the tea plant is considered to be within the fan-shaped area between the Nagaland, Manipur, and Lushai hills along the Assam-Myanmar (Burma) frontier in the west; through to China, probably as far as Zhejiang province in the east; and from this line south through the hills of Myanmar and Thailand into Vietnam. The three main varieties of the tea plant, China, Assam, and Cambodia, each occur in their most distinct form at the extremes of the fan-shaped area. There are an infinite number of hybrids between the varieties; such crosses can be seen in almost any tea field.

- The China variety

Multistemmed bush growing as high as 9 feet (2.75 metres), is a hardy plant able to withstand cold winters and has an economic life of at least 100 years. When grown at an altitude near that of Darjiling (Darjeeling) and Sri Lanka (Ceylon), it produces teas with valuable flavour during the season's second flush or growth of new shoots.

- The Assam variety

A single-stem tree ranging from 20 to 60 feet (6 to 18 metres) in height and including several subvarieties, has an economic life of 40 years with regular pruning and plucking. The tea planter recognizes five main subvarieties: the tender light-leaved Assam, the less tender dark-leaved Assam, the hardy Manipuri and Burma types, and the very large-leaved Lushai. In Upper Assam the dark-leaved Assam plant, when its leaves are highly pubescent, produces very fine quality "golden tip" teas during its second flush. (The Chinese word pekho, meaning "white hair" or "down," refers to the "tip" in tea, which is correlated with quality.)

- The Cambodia variety,

The Cambodia variety a single-stem tree growing to about 16 feet (5 metres) in height, is not cultivated but has been naturally crossed with other varieties.

The mature leaves of the tea plant, differing in form according to variety, range from 1.5 to 10 inches (3.8 to 25 cm) in length, the smallest being the China variety and the largest the Lushai subvariety. In harvesting, or plucking, the shoot removed usually includes the bud and the two youngest leaves.

The weight of 2,000 freshly plucked China bush shoots may be 1 pound (0.45 kg); the same number of Assam shoots may weigh 2 pounds (0.9 kg). Tea leaves may be serrated, bullate, or smooth; stiff or flabby; the leaf pose ranges from erect to pendant; and the degree of pubescence varies widely from plant to plant.

Camellia sinensis Leaves Growing

- Cultivation

Tea plants don't really need a feed, just plenty of water, but if you do need to give them a feed, use an ericaceous food and do not harvest that plant for 12-20 days after the next flush, as the taste of the feed will come through the tea leaves. Tea plants can grow to around 2 metres tall. When planting more than one sapling in the ground, leave a distance of 1.5 metres between the plants. This will give room for the plants to breathe and for them to become bushy.

A suitable climate has a minimum annual rainfall of 45 to 50 inches (1,140 to 1,270 mm), with proper distribution. If there is a cool season, with average temperatures 20 °F (11 °C) or more below those of the warm season, the growth rate will decrease and a dormant period will follow, even when the cool season is the wetter one.

Tea soils must be acid; tea cannot be grown in alkaline soils. A desirable pH value is 5.8 to 5.4 or less. A crop of 1,500 pounds of tea per acre (1,650 kg per hectare) requires 1.5 to 2 workers per acre (3.7 to 4.9 workers per hectare) to pluck the tea shoots and perform other fieldwork. Mechanical plucking has been tried but, because of its lack of selectivity, cannot replace hand plucking.

Scientific study of tea production began about 1890. Most tea-producing countries maintain scientific research stations to study every aspect of the subject, including seed production, clonal selection (for the propagation of single leaf cuttings), tea nursery management, transplanting, development of the bush and subsequent pruning and plucking, soil management and fertilizer use, and the ultimate replanting of the stand. Although procedures in all countries are related, appropriate details must be determined for each area. Since 1900, advancements in tea cultivation have increased the average yield per acre in Assam from 400 to 1,000 pounds (180 to 450 kg), with many estates producing over 1,500 pounds (680 kg).

- Growing Tea From Seed

Growing tea from seed is not an exact science and with a germination time of up to 8 weeks, it's not the fastest way to host your first tea party! However, if you fancy giving it a whirl, buy your tea seeds from a reputable trader and ensure that the variety supplied is the Chinese Camellia Sinensis Sinensis and not the Indian Camellie Sinensis Assamica, which needs tropical conditions to thrive.

- Nursery

Vegetative propagation is carried out for clonal multiplication while biclonal seed stocks are propagated through seeds. The tea nursery should be located near a perennial water source. An over head 'pandal' is raised on which a coir mat with 6 mm2 mesh is spread so as to allow about 33% sunlight at midday into the nursery.

Polythene sleeves with a dimension of 30×10 cm are used for filling up the sandy loam/clayey loam soils. The lower three-fourths of the sleeves may be filled with jungle top soil with appropriate proportions of sand to make it a sandy loam. The top one-fourth portion of the sleeve should be filled with the rooting medium. Both the soils should have a pH of 4.5 to 4.8 and EC below 0.05 dsm-1.

One leaf and an internodal cutting with an axillary bud prepared from the 'aperiodic shoots' arising from pruned tea bush is planted in the nursery sleeve and covered with a polythene sheet of 400 guage. April / May and August / September are the most suitable months for planting in nursery. Single nodal cuttings and the grafted plants are prone to Pestalotia attack for the first to six weeks after planting. Contact fungicides like mancozeb at the rate of 30 g in 10 litres may be applied for protecting the rooting cuttings from Pestalotia attack. The plants are allowed to grow for 6-8 months in the nursery and then transferred to the open space for hardening. Hardened nursery plants are transplanted in the field.

- Planting

Should be carried out in the month of June where the areas receiving south-west monsoon and during August in the north east monsoon zones. About 13,000 plants are planted in one hectare following double hedge system of planting (spacing: 135 X 75 X 75 cm). One year old plants are planted in pits with a dimension of 30 X 45 cm. The selected plants for planting should have 14 to 16 healthy mature leaves and the root system should have reached the bottom end of the sleeves at the time of planting. The stem at the collar region should be about pencil thick and brown. Soil and water conservation measures must be adopted while new planting is taken up.

- Training Of Young Tea

Three to four months after planting, apical dominance is arrested by cutting off the leader stem. This operation, called centering (or decentring), promotes the growth of axillary buds and lateral branches are formed. All the plants should be centered as low as possible leaving 8 – 10 healthy mature leaves. For further lateral branch formation, good spread and establishment of plucking surface the growing branches are trained by two stage tipping. First tipping is carried out at 35 cm followed by second tipping at 50 cm.

Formative pruning (branch formation pruning) is carried out at the end of five years after planting. The recommended pruning height for formative pruning is around 45 cm above ground level. At the time of formative pruning branches which are less than pencil size thick are removed.

- Propagation Of Tea Seeds

First, soak your tea seeds in water for between 24 and 48 hours. This allows the seeds to absorb as much water as it can and help to kick start the germination process. In general the seeds that sink give the highest chances of successful germination, although this is by no means guaranteed.

Once removed from the water, place in a seed tray in a warm, sunny position and spray to keep damp. Allow the seeds to come back to air temperature and then cover over with an inch of coarse vermiculite.

- Germination

Keep the soil moist and in a warm, sunny position, hopefully, germination will occur 6-8 weeks later. Once germination of your tea seeds has occurred and the plants have developed 3 or 4 leaves, it is time to separate them into pots using ericaceous compost. Move to a warm, but partially shaded position, spray regularly to keep the soil moist but not wet.

- Shade

Grevillea robusta Commonly called as Silver Oak is the recommended shade tree for tea in south India. The finely dissected leaves facilitate filtering of light and the deep root system does not compete with tea for nutrients. The tree is also suitable for pollarding and periodical lopping to regulate shade.

Grevillea trees can also support the growth of pepper which is intercropped with tea. Grevillea plants are planted at 6.1 X 6.1 m spacing at the time of planting and thinned out at 12.2 X 6.1 m at the end of fifth year and latter on at 12.2 X 12.2 m at the end of ninth or tenth year. The trees are pollarded at a height of 7.6 m in estates located in high elevation and at 9.1

m in mid elevation regions. The trees are also annually lopped before the onset of the monsoon season.

In south -west monsoon zones lopping should be carried out during April/May and the north-east monsoon season in August. Grevillea trees require a pH of around 6.0. therefore, application of 450 to 900 g dolomite lime is recommended to be applied in the planting pits depending upon the initial soil pH.

- Pruning

Pruning is carried out to keep the bushes continuously under vegetative stage. A pruning cycle of four years is recommended for the fields located in low and mid elevation areas and it is five years for the fields in high elevation. Generally a cut across pruning at 60-65 cm is followed depending upon the branch thickness. Formative of pruning is recommended at the end of five years after planting. Generally formative pruning is carried out at about 45 -50 cm from the ground level.

- Tipping

In 'Assam' jat fields, the tipping in material should be four leaves and a bud; Three tiers of leaves may be left above the pruning cut in fields pruned at 55 – 60 cm. Two tiers of leaves may be left above the pruning cut if the bushes were pruned at 60 – 75 cm. For "China" jat fields pruned at 55 – 75 cm, the tipping in material should be four leaves and a bud leaving two tiers of leaves above the pruning cut.

- Mechanization

Cultural operations such as pitting, pruning and harvesting are now being mechanized. We recommend the use of machines for increasing the productivity of the workers. The STIHL BT 120 C earth auger can increase the productivity of the worker nearly three times when compared to manual pitting. Pruning machines with spinning discs are nearly four times more efficient than the manual pruning with knives. One man and two men operated harvesters can increase the productivity four fold.

- Weed Control

The most common grass weeds in south Indian tea fields are Axonopus compressus (Sw.) P.Beauv (Carpet grass), Digitaria adscendens [HBK] Henr. (Crab grass), D.longiflora Pers (Finger grass), Panicum repens L.(Couch grass/Ginger grass), Paspalum conjugatum Berg(Buffalo grass). The common dicot weeds are, Ageratum conyzoides L. (Goat weed), Bidens biternata (Lour) Merr. & Shreff. (Spanish needle), Crassocephalum crepidioides (Benth) Moore. (Pile wort), Conyza ambigua DC, Mitracarpus verticillatus (Schum. & Thonn.)Vatke.

Backpack sprayers fitted with WFN 0.024, 0.040 and VLV-50 nozzles are used for spraying the recommended herbicides. Both the pre and post emergence herbicides are useful to control the weeds in tea fields. Pre emergence herbicides such as diuron and oxyfluorfen can be applied in young tea fields and in the pruned tea fields. The contact post emergence herbicide like paraquat is useful to control the weeds during the monsoon seasons.

The translocated type of herbicides such as glyphosate and 2, 4-D can be sprayed during the pre and post monsoon seasons. For the control of mixed population of weeds with predominant infestation of broad leaved weeds glyphosate + 2, 4 -D + a non – ionic wetting agent at the rate of 1.75 litres

+ 1.40 kg + 0.50 litres in 450 litres of water / ha is recommended. For the control of grasses glyphosate + kaolin + a non – ionic wetting agent at the rate of 2.0 litres + 2.00 kg + 0.50 litres / ha is recommended. Alternately paraquat at the rate of 1.5 litres / ha can be sprayed for the control of soft weeds or the same herbicides at the rate of 2.25 litres /ha can be sprayed for the control of hardy weeds. Ammonium salt of glyphosate (Excel Mera 71) is also recommended at 30 g /10 L of water for weed control.

- Pests And Diseases

The tea plant is subject to attack from at least 150 insect species and 380 fungus diseases. In northeast India, where 125 pests and 190 fungi have been detected, losses from pests and diseases have been estimated at 67 million pounds (30 million kg) of tea per annum. More than 100 pests and 40 diseases occur in the tea fields of Japan. Sri Lanka, where estates are close together or contiguous, has recorded many blights and suffered serious losses. Africa has little trouble with blights; the tea mosquito (Helopeltis theivora) is the only serious pest. The Caucasus, with a climate similar to that of

Japan, grows the China variety of plant and has no serious pests or blights.

- Harvesting Camellia sinensis

Tea plants are generally dormant in Winter months. So Spring should bring evidence of new growth in the first 'flush' of tea shoots. Pluck the first two bright green leaves and the bud from each branch using finger and thumb, this should be easy to do with a gentle pluck. Regular harvesting like this encourages further growth and helps to create a more bushy shrub. These young, apple green leaves are then ready to be brewed into a calming cup of tea.

Young tea fields and the fields immediately after pruning is to be hand plucked irrespective of the season. Fields that had crossed more than 15 months from pruning can be harvested with the help of hand held shears. Shear harvesting increases the productivity of the workers. Hand held motorised harvesters have been evaluated and found useful to achieve high labour productivity. Both the one man and two men operated motorized harvesters are useful in tea fields planted on moderate and gentle slopes. The battery operated harvesters are also useful to increase the productivity of the women pluckers. During the drought season of December to March addition of a new tier of maintenance foliage is recommended by hand plucking to a mother leaf. Plucking interval for hand plucking may vary from 9 to 13 days in different seasons while it ranges from 15 to 18 days for shear harvesting.

Harvesting of the tea plant can occur several times throughout the more vigorous growing period of spring to summer, and this gives plenty of opportunity to try different methods of creating your preferred tea. The same plant, Camellia sinensis, gives rise to several different teas: Green Tea, Oolong Tea and Black Tea. The difference between them is down to the processes the leaves undergo once harvested.

Turning your home grown harvested tea leaves into a lovely cup of tea only takes a few steps, have a look at the tea production process.

Other Tea plants

Chamomile

Chamomile is known for its calming effects, but the small, daisy-like flower can also increase appetite and relieve indigestion. The two most popular varieties of chamomile are German and Roman. German chamomile is more suited to small gardens or planters, while Roman chamomile makes a good ground cover.

Sow chamomile seeds indoors or in the garden. Chamomile grows easily when allowed to shed mature seeds. Plants do best in fertile, well-drained soil in a sunny spot. While chamomile will grow most places, it will not tolerate temperatures over 98 degrees for very long.

Harvest branches when they have several open flowers, and hang to dry in bunches. Once the stems have dried, remove the blooms and store in an airtight container. To brew, steep two teaspoons of dried flowers in one cup of boiling water for five to 10 minutes.

Mint

Mint is a hardy plant that is fairly easy to care for. It will grow in average soil and partial to full sun. Start seeds indoors and place outside after last frost, or place fresh stem-tip cuttings in moist soil to root. Mint will spread, so plant it near a barrier, such as a sidewalk, or grow it in a container.

Pick leaves often to promote growth and keep the plant bushy. While mint can be dried, it tastes as good fresh. Harvest fresh leaves, tear them up slightly, and steep in boiling water for three to seven minutes, depending on your preference. Learn more about how to grow mint and the health benefits of mint tea.

Mint can be crazy invasive if not contained in the garden, but it makes such great tea that it's totally worth growing it. The only question is what kind of mint to grow. Go to any reputable greenhouse and you'll find an amazing variety of mint flavors, such as:

- Peppermint – high amounts of menthol giving it that intense cool minty flavor
- Spearmint – a sweeter less intense minty flavor, perfect for cooking (eg. Tabbouleh salad)

- Chocolate Mint – truly tastes like chocolate mint wafers
- Apple, Orange, Pineapple, Strawberry or Grapefruit Mint – some are more true to their name than others, great for iced teas
- Mojito Mint – perfect for muddling into ice cold rum tea – aka Mojitos.

Lemon Balm

People have valued lemon balm for its calming properties for centuries. It can also help relieve headaches and lower blood pressure. Lemon balm can be grown from a root clump and is best transferred from early spring to early summer. Start seedlings safely indoors late in the winter, and set them out in spring.

While lemon balm grows easily in most places, it tends to spread. To prevent spread, grow this herb in a pot, or cut back flowering stems in late summer. Lemon balm grows best in rich, well-drained soil and full sun. Its leaves are best when harvested just as flowers are beginning to bloom. For tea, steep a few fresh leaves in boiling water for two to five minutes.

Lavender

Lavender produces beautiful purple flowers that not only smell and taste wonderful, but also help ease headaches and prevent fainting and dizziness. Lavender prefers very well-drained, almost sandy, soil and sunny, open areas. It can grow in pots or planters, but will grow taller and have better air circulation in a garden, which will help deter fungus.

Plant seeds in late summer or early autumn, or split and plant existing clumps in autumn. Harvest stalks of lavender just as flowers bloom, and dry in small bundles before storing in an airtight container. To brew, steep four teaspoons of dried flowers in boiling water for two to five minutes.

Echinacea

Echinacea has antiviral and antibacterial properties, which make it great for helping to combat colds and sore throats. The whole echinacea plant, from its purple coneflowers to its roots, can be used in tinctures and teas. Start with a plant from a nursery, or sow seeds indoors in late winter. Echinacea will not bloom reliably until its second year, but it is hardy and can withstand cold winters. It prefers full sun in cold climates and partial shade in areas with hot summers. Echinacea grows best in rich soil with a neutral pH.

 Roots can be washed, cut into small pieces, and dried. Stems should be cut above the bottom set of leaves and hung upside down to dry. To brew echinacea tea, steep one tablespoon of dried root or dried stems and flowers in one cup of boiling water for three minutes.

Hibiscus

Hibiscus tea has a very tangy flavor and a rich red color. Like with several other herbal teas, when you brew hibiscus you are actually brewing the flower. Studies show that it can measurably lower blood pressure. It is also frequently used for stomach upset, cramps, fever and sore throat. It's rich in vitamin C so it can help to boost your body's immune system.

Giant Hyssop (Agastache Foeniculum)

This tall purple beauty is probably my favorite tea herb. It's gorgeous, easy to grow, attractive to pollinators and tastes delicious! As a native North American prairie species, it's perfect for northern gardens as it is quite drought tolerant and will come back year after year despite long cold winters. While it does reseed itself and it is a member of the mint family, giant hyssop is not aggressively invasive, it's easy to pull out if it's where you don't want it. I think you'll love the light sweet black licorice flavor.

Lemon Grass (Cymbopogon)

Use lemon grass as a tall grassy center piece in large planters. Not only does it look great, but when you rub it, you'll get a lemony scent that is suppose to help deter mosquitoes. I'm not convinced about the mosquito repellent properties, but I love the flavor of lemon grass tea! I've never been able to grow thick stalks like the kind you buy to cook with, like in Thai cooking, but I get plenty of long grassy blades that are perfect for tea. It really does taste like lemon grass – the longer you steep it, the more pronounced it gets. I like mixing lemon grass with dried fruit for tasty herbal fruit tea combinations. full lemon grass

Lemon Balm (Melissa Officinalis)

Here's another lemony flavored herb that's great for tea making. But, be warned, it's a member of the mint family, so it's another aggressive perennial that spreads via seeds and runners. It's best to restrain it in a container. Enjoy the refreshing lemony scent and flavor of this plant all summer long with repeated harvests. Hot or cold, fresh or dried, it makes great tea. Here's an article on harvesting and drying lemon or lime balm.

Lemon Verbena (Aloysia Citrodora)

You won't believe the lemony scent from this woody herb. This perennial tropical shrub won't survive anything cooler than Zone 8, so it may be a little more challenging to find in prairie garden centres – but if you do, pick one up and plan to keep it indoors over the winter. It grows quickly in our hot summers so you'll enjoy multiple harvests. The strong lemony flavor can be used in place of lemon zest in baking, glazes, infused vinegar and in tea. Use it on its own or in a fruity herbal tea blend.

Borage (Borago Officinalis)

With it's incredibly stunning edible flowers and ability to attract pollinators borage is a must in any garden. The flowers and bristly leaves taste remarkably similar to cucumbers; as such, they're perfect for making flavored water – just like at the spa. You can also use them in iced teas and lemonades. While we've never made hot tea with borage, it can be done. We also use chopped borage leaves and whole flowers in salads. The plant is quite bushy and floppy, about the size of a tomato plant. Borage is an annual that reseeds easily. Luckily, managing volunteer borage is very easy as they can be hoed or pulled easily.

Lemon Thyme (Thymus Citriodorus)

Did you know that many savory herbs like rosemary, sage and parsley make excellent tea as well?! It's true. Their flavor is perhaps a little too intense to serve as an afternoon tea, but they're certainly drinkable and worth researching for their medicinal properties. Out of the culinary herbs I grow, I most enjoy lemon thyme as tea. Lemon thyme grows back every year (it may need replacing after 5 or more years), makes a beautiful ground cover, tastes great on fish, chicken or veggies AND it makes a lovely light lemony flavored tea.

One final plant that makes my top list of tea herbs, and certainly there are many more herbs that can be made into tea, is stevia. It's not that stevia makes a delicious tea on its own, it's that it makes a fantastic sweetener for any tea. Stevia, also known as the sugar plant, is super sweet and just a tiny bit will sweeten an entire tea pot. I prefer using a tiny bit of dried, crumbled stevia leaves instead of fresh leaves for sweetening tea. Unlike store bought stevia powder which is white, homemade dried stevia is green and has a slight aftertaste. It's worth a try, especially if you're trying to cut back on sugar.

Conclusion.

Take your time with layout and planning, because while a tea garden should be functional, it should also be beautiful. As you sketch out layout ideas in the available space you have, you can start to see what shape the garden will take so you can decide what to plant where; this will allow you to start building beds, adding soil, and thinking about the placement of decorative pavers and other elements.